How to Find the Right Church

How to Find the Right Church

A COMPLETE GUIDE

DONALD THOMAS

fivesolaspress

Literature for your joy and God's glory

Dedication

To my fellow Christian sojourners in your pursuit of God's will for the right church.

Contents

Acknowledgments

I NEVER CEASE TO BE amazed at the seemingly endless list of scrolling credits that follow a movie. In gratitude, the film makers meticulously acknowledge the hundreds of people that it took to produce a brief ninety minutes of entertainment.

Let me scroll through a few of the behind-the-scenes people for whose help and encouragement I am gratefully indebted:

John MacArthur, whose preaching ministry early in my Christian walk gave me a growing love for the local church;

The many preachers of old whose timeless writings continue to shape the life and ministry of today's church;

The elders and congregation of Trinity Bible Church;

Ed Eubanks, a new friend I have yet to meet, Tim Feathers, and Karista Low, who laboriously applied their editorial skills and insights into the project;

Acknowledgments

Finally, a very deep personal thanks to my wife Mary whose sacrificial life and ministry have been a great source of blessing for the last forty-six years of marriage.

Preface

"WHY DON'T WE START ATTENDING church?"

After seven years of marriage, my wife Mary shocked me one day with this suggestion. At first her request fell on deaf ears: I thought if I just ignored her it would go away— after all, neither of us had a churched background. At the time, I was attending law school in Chicago and working two part-time jobs; Sunday was the only day of the week that I could catch up on sleep and slip in a little tennis.

Mary was persistent. Until then, the only time we had attended church was the day of our wedding. Neither of us had a clue what to look for in a church; I couldn't have articulated the difference between a Buddhist and a Baptist. But in a moment of weakness, I caved in.

That first Sunday we started with the church that was within walking distance of our apartment: a mainline denominational church that met in a drab-looking brick building with white antebellum pillars framing the front door. Strangers in a strange land, we sat on a hard oak pew in the back row. I have a faint memory of singing a few hymns out of a musty-smelling hymnal; after reciting the

Preface

Lord's Prayer, we endured a short homily that had more in common with a sociology class than the Scriptures. The final amen was the cue for everyone to exit, which reminded me of a crowd of movie-goers robotically leaving a theater. No one greeted us or acknowledged our presence, and we left with a sense of emptiness.

Several more false starts followed, leaving me certain of one thing: if this is what going to church was like, I didn't want anything to do with it. Finally, one Saturday I opened the Chicago Yellow Pages to the "church" section, closing my eyes and running my finger down the column to about halfway. When I opened my eyes, my finger was pointing to a church in Naperville, more than fifteen miles from our home. I stubbornly told Mary, "If this doesn't work out, neither of us are to mention going to church again!" Little did we know that the kindness of a sovereign God had guided my finger to stop on that little church in Naperville where we would hear the gospel, be wonderfully saved, and grow in the early days of our Christian walk.

Our journey is certainly not a model to follow, but I share it as an illustration of the importance of knowing what to look for in a search for a new church. When there are no guideposts in the pursuit of a new church, it is easy to feel adrift with nothing more than fleeting emotions and vain imaginations as guidance. The good news is that the same God who saves his people and places them in his church does not leave them alone to figure out which local church they should attend; throughout the New Testament, he has given the clear marks of a biblically sound and ordered church to guide his sheep to the right flock.

Whenever visitors have come through our church doors,

I have made inquiry as to what they are looking for in a church. Many, if not most, have been just like Mary and me, without a clue.

Recently, a single mom came to church with her son. She was new to the community and searching for a church "like the one back home." When asked about the beliefs and practices of her previous church, she bowed her head and said, "All I know is that it was the place where we learned about Jesus."

Some have walked into our midst because they felt drawn by the welcoming sign outside. Others have indicated they were looking for a program-driven church filled with activities for their children. Other prospective visitors have inquired if we have a "Spirit-filled" worship service. When pressed, however, most are unable to articulate any doctrinal non-negotiables. Most visitors appear to be searching for a church like they would shop for a new pair of shoes: it must be just the right fit, and above all it must feel good.

As I have grown in my love for the church, I have come to see her as the beautiful bride that Jesus loves, died for, and now heads. Christians are not free to turn the local church into a den of self-pleasure; rather, it is the gathering of his blood-bought flock, with the overarching goal of glorifying God and delighting in him forever. Anyone who is looking for a new church should search for one that faithfully pursues this ultimate end.

It is my joy to offer this guide through the Scriptures for those essential marks that will help you discern the right church. As you read, keep the following in mind:

- First, this book will serve as a personal handbook to aid in your search. Use it as a travel guide of sorts:

when you find yourself in a time of church transition, it can serve as a personal guide to find the right fit.

- Second, I have kept each chapter fairly concise; if anything provokes you to dig a little deeper, a recommended reading list is included at the end of each chapter.

- Third, there is no perfect church this side of eternity, and most churches are located in small towns where your options may be few. You might not find a church that meets all the marks listed in this book.

- Fourth, the process of finding the right church will require you to understand the principles found in this book, and inquire of their presence with the leadership of each church under consideration. A list of suggested interview questions is included with each chapter to help you through this inquiry.

- Fifth, it is helpful to teach these principles to your children, helping them to understand why you select a certain church. You will be equipping them with the resources to find the right church for themselves when they leave home.

- Lastly, this book is intended to serve as a resource for churches to share with visitors as a helpful tool to guide them in their search for a church home.

May God direct your steps as he leads you to a place of spiritual growth and happiness, unto his glory!

CHAPTER 1
A Time to Join and a Time to Leave

For everything there is a season,
and a time for every matter under heaven.
- *Ecclesiastes 3:1*

SOLOMON'S WORDS ABOUT THE GOD-ORDAINED time for everything under heaven raise two practical questions: is there a "right" time to join a church—as well as a time to leave it? If so, when is the right time?

You might be a new Christian, wondering whether you should step out and join a church. Or maybe you have just left a church and are seeking a new one. Regardless of the reasons, it can be overwhelming to embark on a quest for a church. Before we consider the proper time for leaving a church, it is important to answer the question: when is the time to join a church?

The Bible clearly teaches that there is a right time to join a local church. Upon salvation you become a member of the universal church, the body of Christ (1 Cor. 12:13); every believer in Christ is also to formally commit to membership in a local church, an identifiable body of believers.

Joining with a local church is not an option—it is a matter of obedience to God's plan for your life in Christ! The writer to the Hebrews commands believers to be part of a local body for this purpose: "And let us consider how to stir up one another to love and good works, not neglecting to meet together, as is the habit of some, but encouraging one another, and all the more as you see the Day drawing near" (Heb. 10:24–25).

When is the right time to join a church? Immediately upon trusting in Jesus Christ as your Savior. This is God's purpose—for your spiritual good, and for his glory.

This gives way to the second question: when is the right time to leave a church? This question is important to consider, not least because we live in a time when church affiliation is taken very lightly. It's become common for professing Christians to migrate like birds from church to church.

Joining a local body of believers is a covenant commitment to cleave to that church family with a similar intensity and resolve as that which married couples embody in their commitment to one another. We are to bond together for our mutual edification and accountability. It is a spiritual relationship which no believer should casually walk away from.

There are, however, several situations in which it is the right time to leave one church and join another. The first is when God providentially changes life circumstances, resulting in a change of community. Life is full of changes which may involve a move; a few examples include the loss of a spouse; commencement of (or graduation from) college; a new job; and entering into military service.

However, too often everything is factored into a decision to move except for the presence of a good church. It's not uncommon for people to leave good churches lured by salary, climate, and/or recreation without first considering what church will be waiting for them when they move. Every opportunity to relocate should always be prayerfully considered in light of the impact that move would have on church affiliation. A close family member recently turned down a lucrative job offer that would have required his family to relocate. He prayerfully counted the cost of doubling his income with the effect the move would have on his church life. Because the church opportunities in the new community were minimal, he decided that increasing his income did not outweigh leaving a loving fellowship where he served as an elder.

Secondly, you should separate from a church when it departs from its essential beliefs and practices. The Reformers wrestled over the question: "What are the essential elements of a true church?" They reduced them to three central marks—the sound preaching of the Word of God, the faithful administration of the sacraments, and the diligent practice of church discipline. Whenever a church departs from any of these essential marks, it is time to prayerfully consider leaving.

Regrettably, there are always churches abandoning the faithful preaching and teaching of sound doctrine (Gal. 1:7–9). Doctrinal anemia is widespread; congregations that once stood firm on biblical inerrancy no longer rest on the Word of God alone as their sole source of faith and practice. The gospel that teaches repentance and the Lordship of Christ has been reduced to a sentimental "easy-believism."

We read of more and more congregations ordaining homosexuals and ministers officiating at same-sex marriages.

That said, you should not leave a church over minor doctrinal differences; there will be minor disagreements at any church you attend. A helpful saying attributed to Aurelius Augustine, and repeated by the Puritan Richard Baxter, strikes the right balance: "In essentials unity, in non-essentials liberty, in all things charity."

Before you leave a church for doctrinal reasons, be sure that you are behaving as a good Berean would have (Acts 17:10–12): carefully study the doctrine in question; go to your church leadership and discuss the matter with a humble, teachable spirit. This provides an opportunity to clarify the church's position, as well as helping you see if there is any error in your own doctrinal understanding. Should the church be found in error, call its leadership to repentance, humbly but confidently; if they see the error of their ways and return to embracing doctrinal truth, you have done much to strengthen the church and maintain her purity, unity, and peace. If there is no repentance, then you are free to depart.

Likewise, it is time to leave a church when it has seriously departed from the faithful observance of the ordinances of the church, also called the sacraments. Christ gave to his church the two ordinances of Baptism and the Lord's Supper. He ordained his church to baptize new converts, and to regularly break bread in remembrance of Jesus Christ. It might become necessary to separate from a church that alters the meaning or refuses to faithfully administer the ordinances of the church. Although such departures from orthodoxy are rare, they aren't unheard of; I read of a large church that changed its belief and practice of admitting professing believers to receive the Lord's Supper ("credocommunion"—communion based upon professed belief) to allowing small infants who have yet to confess faith in Christ to partake in the sacrament ("paedocommunion"—the admittance of baptized children to the communion table).

Finally, it will be time to leave a church that rejects the pursuit of holiness by not faithfully observing the God-given means of church discipline (Matt. 18:15–20). Christ died to make his church holy, without spot or wrinkle (Eph. 5:25–27). For the spiritual welfare of your soul and the souls of your family, you must separate from a church that refuses to confront unrepentant sin. A church that neglects the sins of its members is a church that will quickly be turned to a den of devils.

Is there ever a time not to leave a church? In my years of ministry I have witnessed more people leaving churches for relational reasons rather than doctrinal ones. It seems that many professing believers have a greater tolerance for false teachers than they do for teachers who seem to them to be "unfriendly."

Frequently when I ask visitors why they are leaving their church, I receive answers like: "They're an unfriendly bunch," "No one ever says hello to me," or, "That church lacks joy." They usually are surprised by my response; rather than receiving my sympathy, I encourage them to return to their church and work through their relational problems. They have entered into a covenant relationship with their church; they must keep that covenant.

That's what life in the body of Christ is all about. We are called to live out the gospel that we embrace. I explain to them that if they can't live in harmony in their former church they will not find harmony in a new church—they will take their heart with them wherever they go (for those who need help in resolving relational conflict I point them to an excellent book by Ken Sande, *The Peacemaker**).

God is most glorified when his church is living out a collective life of redemption in love and unity before a fallen world. There is a time to join a church, and a time to leave one. God will guide you in his timetable as you prayerfully follow his footsteps.

---

* Ken Sande, *The Peacemaker: A Biblical Guide to Resolving Personal Conflict* (Grand Rapids, MI: Baker Book House, 1991).

CHAPTER 2
A Pathway to Follow

In all your ways acknowledge him,
and he will make straight your paths.
~ Proverbs 3:6

FINDING THE RIGHT CHURCH REQUIRES more than a random luck of the draw. There is a jungle out there, filled with all types of churches; some are poisonous and can be deadly to your spiritual well-being. Many lack the spiritual nutrition to promote growth and vitality in your Christian life. In the mix there are also good churches that are committed to faithfully shepherding your soul, with the goal that you might be found without spot or wrinkle at the return of Jesus Christ.

Cutting your way through the jungle requires due diligence on your part. You may find the following steps profitable in leading you into a church that will be a healthy spiritual home and community for you.

Research

First, begin by doing your homework. Prior to the widespread adoption of the Internet, the only way of learning about a church was to visit and pick up any literature that could be found. One could easily invest several months investigating the basic beliefs and practices of the churches in their community. The Internet has greatly streamlined the process.

Begin by making a list of all the churches in your community via a basic search. From that list, make a shorter list of potential churches that you would like to know more about—perhaps because of their denominational affiliation, or because you have heard of them from fellow believers. Then go to the web page of each of these churches, mining as much information as you can from each site. Search for the following on each page:

- **Statement of Faith.** A written statement of church doctrinal beliefs is variously labeled as: "doctrinal statement," "confession of faith," "what we believe," or something similar. (In the next chapter we'll discuss the importance of this statement of faith.) You must be willing to dig deep in order to learn the doctrines the church embraces—in fact, a statement of faith is so essential to your search that, if the church does not offer one in writing, you should skip over it and move on to the next church on your list. Make sure their statement is an accurate statement of biblical truth. Generally, a lengthier, more detailed statement is a better record of what a church believes and teaches than a shorter, more minimalistic statement. *

---

*   An exception to this general principle is if a church offers a brief summary, followed by a link to a document or another website that is more comprehensive in scope.

- **Mission Statement.** A mission statement, sometimes entitled something like "statement of purpose" or "about our church," is an abbreviated declaration of what the church understands to be its purpose of existence. A good mission statement might avow that the church's overarching chief end is to "glorify God and enjoy him forever" (1 Cor. 10:31). It may also include various biblical ways it seeks to glorify God, such as faithfully proclaiming the gospel to the nations of the world, equipping the members for service, building up the church into the image of Christ, and worshiping God.
- **Church Distinctives.** This is a brief list of what the church considers to be its primary areas of emphasis or uniqueness—what sets it apart from the other churches around it. In some cases, this list may be attached to, or even intermingled with, the congregation's mission statement. Here you will find brief descriptions about its programs, worship, and preaching; this might help you distinguish this church from others on your list. Ask yourself: do these distinctions describe a church that is God-centered, or one that is man-centered?
- **Church Leadership.** What leadership offices does the church have? Read any biographical sketches of the church office bearers. What is their educational background and ministry experience? How are they involved in the leadership of the congregation? Does the leadership appear to be a good representation of

the congregation as a whole?**

- **Online Sermons.** You can learn much about the preaching ministry of the church even before you attend, by listening to a few sermons online. We had a family visit our church that was prayerfully considering relocating to Wyoming from Maryland. Before their first visit, they knew more about our church and its preaching ministry than some of our local visitors! Sermons are often catalogued on the church web page, or linked to a website such as sermonaudio.com or YouTube. Remember, you are not listening for someone that measures up to your favorite radio preacher; often these are men who are uniquely gifted for a broader ministry. Instead, listen for a man (or men, if there is more than one pastor) who labors faithfully in the study of the Bible to richly feed the flock of God. Does the pastor preach biblical sermons? Is there doctrinal depth to the sermons? Can you hear passion and a love for God's Word and his people in the pastor's preaching?

Which One?

Next, after finishing your homework, prioritize your findings. This will help you narrow your search down to the top two or three churches. Plan to visit each of these churches. Then, arrive early enough to attend Sunday school classes, if they are offered, and greet the people; during the worship service, listen carefully to the preaching. Does it edify the

---

** It may be difficult, or even impossible, to assess this last question without first visiting the church; still, it will be an important one to keep in mind during further exploration.

saints and evangelize the lost? Join wholeheartedly in the singing, and pay attention to the various elements of the worship service. Is the whole service marked by reverence? Is it more man-centered entertainment or God-centered praise? Does it represent the gospel in every way possible? Following the service, stay and greet the people; is there a warm welcome for visitors?

If you are to truly learn about a church, you must visit more than just one Sunday worship service: attend other church gatherings such as prayer meetings, fellowship gatherings and midweek Bible studies. There you will discover more about the life and ministry of the church, as you interact with God's people. Likewise, return for a second or a third Sunday, and note what, if anything, is different.

Following this, if you remain interested in the church you've been considering, meet with and interview the pastor(s) and officers of the church. (Freely use the suggested questions that you will find at the end of each chapter that follows this one.) If there is more than one officer in the church, try to speak with each one separately—you can quickly discern if they share the same vision and beliefs, and you will also discover their unique giftings and callings.

Mary and I recently had a visiting couple over for lunch after worship, and they brought with them a lengthy list of questions about our church. As I answered their last question, the couple looked at each other and broke out in laughter. I asked them if it was something I said, to which the husband replied, "These are the same questions I asked another elder and you both gave the exact same answers. Do you have a script that you both memorized?" I assured him there was no such script; instead, it underscored the blessing of the unity that exists in our leadership.

Pray!

Finally, commit your quest for the right church to the Lord in prayer. Ask for God's guidance throughout this important process. As you do, also pray for the churches you are considering, asking that God would grant them the strength to remain faithful to him in their ministries, and that you might find a healthy church home among them. Pray for the leaders of these churches, and for the growth of their members; pray that God would use them to expand his kingdom, and that new believers would be brought into the church through their ministries.

As you pray, trust that God is at work in you and in your search, and rest in the Good Shepherd's care for his sheep—that he will tend you safely into the fold of his flock that he is already preparing for you!

CHAPTER 3
The Pillar of Truth

If I delay, you may know how one ought to behave in the household of God, which is the church of the living God, a pillar and buttress of the truth.
~ 1 Timothy 3:15

WHAT IS THE MOST IMPORTANT mark of the church, the one that should be at the top of your list in your search for the right congregation? Surprisingly, it is often the one that is least sought after; it is also the first mark mentioned by Luke in the book of Acts, when he described the life and ministry of the New Testament church in Jerusalem: this was a body of believers that was "devoted to the apostles' teaching" (Acts 2:42). Christ has designed his church to be that solid pillar that upholds doctrinal truth (1 Tim. 3:5).

But in our culture, relativism long ago began to replace absolutes. Beware of the church where this aspect of culture has crept in, and the absolutes of Scripture have been explained away or watered down. Look for a church that embraces sound doctrine—and that faithfully preaches, teaches, applies, and defends the truth of God's Word.

Don't be led astray by a church that points to the Bible and tells you they have no other doctrine than Scripture. These will frequently chant a mantra like "doctrine divides and love unites." At first this seems to have an attractive and even spiritual ring. However, the question isn't whether their beliefs are found in the Bible; rather, the question is whether they know and believe what the Holy Spirit intended when he authored the Bible. Many false teachers go to the Bible to support their heresies; they can give you chapter and verse to deny the Trinity, deity of Christ, or salvation by grace alone. It is important that a church knows what it believes about the essential truths of the faith.

Keep in mind that a church that proudly declares that it has no other doctrine than the Bible still has an unwritten statement of faith. It might be the doctrine of the pastor only, or be embraced by a majority of its members. The problem is, it might take you several years of sitting under that pastor's preaching before you know what he actually believes. This problem is compounded by the fact that, every time there is a new pastor in such a church, you will start over with new doctrine!

The church is called to preach and teach *sound* doctrine (Titus 1:9; 2 Tim. 4:3; Jude 1:3). Good teaching directs and stirs our worship of God. Solid theology strengthens us to fight off false teachers who, like ravaging wolves, seek to enter and devour the flock of God (Acts 20:29–31). Right instruction is God's means for our sanctification (John 17:17). Doctrinal truth unites the hearts of God's people and guides the life and ministry of the church. Sound doctrine is the fence that defines fellowship in the gospel ministry. Through it, our very eternal destiny may hang in the balance! Because, without it, we cannot know and believe in the one true God, or in Jesus Christ whom he has sent.

Generally, churches that are weaker in doctrine will provide a brief, anemic statement of faith; sadly, there are many churches whose entire doctrine is summed up on a half-sheet of paper which—although it may say something about God, Jesus, and salvation—leaves unaddressed many of the essential doctrines of the Christian faith.

A doctrinally strong church will generally have a lengthy statement of its beliefs. However, beware: length alone does not always translate into truth and practice. What should be included in a solid statement of faith? Ask yourself, as you read through their doctrinal statement, what the church's understanding is of the following essential doctrines of the Christian faith:

- The nature of God
- The person and work of Christ
- The person and work of the Holy Spirit
- Scripture (including their view on inspiration, inerrancy, and the canon or list of books that comprise the Bible)
- Creation
- The nature of man (including the nature of sin, man's state, and how it affects man's relationship with God)
- Salvation (including justification by faith, sanctification, and glorification)
- Perseverance of the saints
- Last things (including heaven for the saved and eternal hell for the lost)

Beyond these doctrinal essentials, it is helpful if a state-

ment of faith also includes the church's teaching on:
- The church
- Gifts of the Spirit (tongues, healing, etc.)
- The ordinances of Baptism and Lord's Supper
- The Christian Sabbath
- Church polity (government)
- Marriage (as a heterosexual, monogamous, covenantal union for life)

Our church identifies itself as a "confessional" church—by which we mean that we have adopted one of the historical confessions of faith as our doctrinal foundation: the London Baptist Confession of Faith of 1689. It is comprised of thirty-two chapters, each addressing one particular doctrine. This is how C.H. Spurgeon viewed the confession:

> This ancient document is the most excellent epitome of the things most surely believed among us. It is not issued as an authoritative rule or code of faith, whereby you may be fettered, but as a means of edification in righteousness. It is an excellent, though not inspired, expression of the teaching of those Holy Scriptures by which all confessions are to be measured. We hold to the humbling truths of God's sovereign grace in the salvation of lost sinners. Salvation is through Christ alone and by faith alone.

Each time you visit a new church, ask for a copy of their doctrinal statement; a church that holds to one of the historic confessions, such as the London Baptist Confession (Baptist), the Westminster Confession of Faith (Presbyterian), or the Savoy Declaration (Congregationalist), will usually be doctrinally sound although you will find some differences on minor issues. I say *usually* because it is possible for a church to adopt a confession, yet ignore it in practice. A good example is Robert Schuller, the forerunner of the Seeker-Sensitive Movement. Schuller was ordained in the Reformed Church in America (RCA), which held to the Belgic Confession. In practice, however, Schuller abandoned the confession and exchanged theology for therapy: rather than preaching the victory of the cross over sin, he preached the false gospel of positive thinking.

Not every good church is confessional. There are many doctrinally sound churches that have their own detailed written statement of faith.

This raises one final question: how does a person find a church that embraces sound doctrine if they themselves have never learned sound doctrine? Perhaps they are new Christians that have yet to learn the doctrines of the Christian faith. Maybe the only doctrine they know comes from the milk they were fed at their last church. God places on each of our shoulders the responsibility of knowing and growing in the truth of his Word:

> For though by this time you ought to be teachers, you need someone to teach you again the basic principles of the oracles of God. You need milk, not solid food, for everyone who lives on milk is unskilled in the word of righteousness, since he is a child. But solid food is for the mature, for those who have their powers of discernment trained by constant practice to distinguish good from evil (Heb. 5:12–14).

You must avail yourself of all of the God-given means to grow in sound doctrine. If your understanding of Christian doctrine is weaker than you think it should be, I recommend that you pick up one of the many good books that survey Christian doctrine. I have included a recommended list of several such books at the end of this chapter.

As you read through a church's detailed statement of faith, you will quickly learn what that church believes and practices. I recommend that you avoid churches without a doctrinal statement; it is an indication that they may not take doctrine seriously, and without such a statement it will take you a long time to discover the church's beliefs—at which point, it might be too late!

Questions to Ask

1. Does your church have a statement of faith?

2. Does it reflect all of the current beliefs and practices of your church? If not, which ones are not included?

3. What is your final authority for truth and practice?

4. What are your thoughts on the quote, "doctrine divides, whereas love unifies?"

5. Tell me the gospel as this church understands it. (Carefully listen to the answer to see if it contains the following essential elements: repentance, faith in Christ alone, and the ongoing Lordship of Christ).

Digging Deeper

Berkhof, Louis. *Summary of Christian Doctrine.* London: Banner of Truth Trust, 1960.

MacArthur, John and Richard Mayhue, eds. *Biblical Doctrine: A Systematic Summary of Bible Truth.* Wheaton, IL: Crossway, 2017.

Milne, Bruce. *Know the Truth: A Handbook of Christian Belief.* Downers Grove, IL: Tyndale House, 1992.

Sproul, R.C. *Essential Truths of the Christian Faith.* Wheaton, IL: Tyndale House, 1992.

Watson, Thomas. *A Body of Divinity: Contained in Sermons upon the Westminster Assembly's Catechism.* London: Banner of Truth Trust, 1965.

CHAPTER 4
Biblical Leadership

And he gave some as apostles, and some as prophets, and some as evangelists, and some as pastors and teachers, for the equipping of the saints for the work of service, to the building up of the body of Christ;
~ Ephesians 4:11–12

A CHURCH WILL ONLY BE as strong as the men who oversee and serve the flock of God. The New Testament gives much guidance regarding proper church leadership; in fact, Paul the apostle wrote letters with the central topic of God's pattern and qualifications of leadership.

In your pursuit of the right church, you will come across several forms of church government (polity: episcopal, presbyterian, and congregational). Under the episcopal form of government, the local church is part of a hierarchy of clergy who oversee the local churches underneath them. Under the presbyterian form, the leadership authority resides with the elders of each local church. In the congregationally-led churches (whether single- or plural-elder), leadership authority rests with the individual church members. Which is correct?

The churches that you visit should be able to give you a biblical defense of their form of government. Each type of governance has its own inherent strengths and weaknesses. I believe the presbyterian (elder-led) form of government to be the most biblically defensible; I have also found that it best maintains church unity, and promotes godly biblical oversight.

The options of church government might be limited in your community. The emphasis in Scripture is more upon the qualifications of those who lead than the structure of the church government. Therefore, I encourage you to look for a church where the lives of the men who lead measure up scripturally.

The New Testament speaks of two church offices: elder and deacon. The elders (or bishops, depending on the translation of a Greek word) are shepherds and overseers, called to lead and feed the flock of God. They are called in Scripture Christ's "under-shepherds" (1 Pet. 5:1–4). They are described as spiritually mature men who are living examples of Christlikeness to the sheep, and are called to feed the flock through teaching and preaching the Word of God. As good under-shepherds, they must protect the sheep from false teachers (Acts 20:29–30) and faithfully lead the flock in the pathway of God's will and holiness (Acts 20:28).

You may be wondering if the Bible tells us the number of elders that are to lead each local flock. In your search you might find a church with one sole elder/pastor faithfully laboring over the flock or a larger church with a dozen or more. While no fixed number is mentioned in the Bible, we do find a repeated pattern. The New Testament speaks of a *plurality* (a number greater than one) of elders in each local church (Titus 1:5; James 5:14; Acts 14:23; 1 Tim. 5:17).

I have witnessed the blessing of such a plurality over my years of ministry. For one thing, it offers protection from leadership becoming self-willed. I remember visiting a church where, following the worship service, the pastor stood up and declared, "I am the pastor, this is my church; if you don't like it you can leave right now!" He had forgotten that this was *Christ's* blood-bought church.

A plurality also brings the added blessing of God blending men with differing gifts, strengths, and abilities to collectively discern the will of God and lead the congregation accordingly. Our church is currently led by three elders. Each of us has been graced with unique gifting and personalities: one elder is strong in administration, another in the teaching and proclamation of the Word, and the third in caring and counseling. Such a leadership might be labeled spiritually synergistic—or to borrow from Aristotle, "The whole is greater than the sum of its parts."

Don't rule out a church that does not (yet) have a plurality of elders; many good churches are at a stage of development where they only have one elder. Often, especially in newly planted churches, you will find a godly pastor, but God has yet to raise up another qualified elder. What's important is that the church purposes, prepares, and prays for such a plurality.

The second church office is that of deacon. Deacons too have a vital and specific role in the life and the health of the local church: they are called by God to take care of the physical and logistical needs of the church, so that the elders can remain singularly focused in their role of leading and feeding the flock. The deacons' service to the body of Christ includes the administrative and organizational tasks, stewardship over the finances, care of the needy, ushering, and maintenance of the physical properties of the congregation.

Not only should the church be biblically ordered with the offices of elders and deacons, but these office bearers must also meet the detailed qualifications set by God (1 Tim. 3:1–13; Titus 1:6–16). After a quick comparison of the qualifications of both elders and deacons, you will see that they are very similar—except that the elder has the added qualification of being able to teach.

You will also discover the politically incorrect qualification of male leadership. The office of elder is gender-specific. Paul opened his list of qualifications with, "It is a trustworthy statement: if any *man* aspires to the office of overseer" (1 Tim. 3:1, NASB). In the previous chapter, Paul exhorted, "I do not permit a woman to teach or to exercise authority over a man; rather, she is to remain quiet" (1 Tim. 2:12). He also added, "Therefore an overseer must be above reproach, the *husband of one wife*" (1 Tim. 3:2, emphasis added). Be warned that a church that will compromise on this biblical qualification will be a congregation that may compromise in other important areas of doctrine and practice as well.

May the Lord lead you to the church that is ruled well by godly elders and served by faithful deacons. Be sure to make the extra effort to investigate whether these leaders are men who meet the qualifications of 1 Timothy 3:1–13 and Titus1:5–9.

Questions to Ask

1. What are the offices of your church?

2. What qualifications are required for church officers? (Compare their answer with the list of qualifications in 1 Tim. 3 and Titus 1).

3. Explain how your current church officers meet those qualifications.

4. Are the offices of church leadership gender-specific?

5. Describe the decision-making process of your church when changing the direction of the ministry. What role if any does the congregation play?

Digging Deeper

On Elders:

Dickson, David. *The Elder and His Work.* Phillipsburg, NJ: P&R Publishing, 2004.

Eyers, Lawrence R. *The Elders of the Church.* Phillipsburg, NJ: P&R Publishing, 1975.

Strauch, Alexander. *Biblical Eldership: An Urgent Call to Restore Biblical Church Leadership.* Littleton, CO: Lewis and Roth Publishers, 1995.

Van Dam, Cornelius. *The Elder: Today's Ministry Rooted in All of Scripture.* Phillipsburg, NJ: P&R Publishing, 2009.

Biblical Leadership

On Deacons:

Keller, Timothy. *Ministries of Mercy: the Call of the Jericho Road.* Phillipsburg, NJ: P&R Publishing, 1997.

Strauch, Alexander. *The New Testament Deacon: The Church's Minister of Mercy.* Littleton, CO: Lewis and Roth Publishers, 1992.

CHAPTER 5
Worship in Spirit and Truth

But an hour is coming, and now is, when the true worshipers will worship the Father in spirit and truth; for such people the Father seeks to be His worshipers.
- John 4:23

ONE OF THE MOST COMMON questions inquirers ask about our church is: "Tell me about your worship music," or put another way, "What kind of worship do you have?"

I must admit, it grieves me that they don't first ask what we teach or whether the gospel is preached. Instead, they want to know, first and foremost, if the songs we sing are traditional hymns, Old Testament Psalms, or the latest contemporary music. From there, the questions often expand to: what, if any, musical instruments accompany our worship? I have learned over the years that an over-emphasis on personal preferences in music styles often reveals a heart that is more focused on "me" than it is on worshiping God!

All About Me?

This "me-centered" approach to worship has the potential to lead you down the wrong path in your search for a new church. Sometime during the 20th century, worship became redefined exclusively as "music." But worship isn't exclusively music; rather, the work of worship is the act of God's redeemed people rendering to the Triune God all the praise, adoration, thanksgiving, and obedience that is due him. Music plays an important—but not exclusive—role in the heartfelt expression of corporate worship.

"Me-centered" worship is misdirected worship. Worship is not about which music makes you feel good, or which musical instruments you prefer to accompany the music you like. As you search for the right church, your worship compass, if you will, should point you to Christ.

Biblical Worship

What should you look for when it comes to the corporate worship of a potential church? The Puritans joined with the Reformers to provide us with much helpful guidance: they rightly realized that worship is not about what *I* want or what makes *me* feel good, but rather what pleases God. Therefore, God's Word should be our best guide in how we approach him in worship. A preacher of old stated it well: "God disapproves of all modes of worship not expressly sanctioned by his Word."[*]

Jesus told a Samaritan woman alongside a well that "God is spirit, and those who worship him must worship in

---

*   Calvin, John. "The Necessity of Reforming the Church" monergism.com, https://www.monergism.com/thethreshold/sdg/calvin_necessityreform. html (accessed August 1, 2016).

spirit and truth" (John 4:24). In other words, truth should be your guiding light in the worship of God. There are many tragic examples of worshipers who chose to worship *their* way. We read in Genesis 4 how God rejected Cain's offering because it was not brought as he prescribed. Later, both Nadab and Abihu were consumed by God for their offering up to him "strange fire" that was contrary to his will (Lev. 10).

As you search Scripture, you find God has prescribed the following elements of worship: reading the Bible (1 Tim. 4:13); biblical preaching (2 Tim. 4:2); singing—though not a particular style of music (Eph. 5:19); prayer (Matt. 21:13); and the faithful observance of the ordinances of baptism and the Lord's Supper (Matt. 28:19; Acts 2:38–39; 1 Cor. 11:23–26). You will not find any references to such contemporary elements as dramatic presentations, puppet shows, or sermonettes aimed exclusively at the little children to the exclusion of the congregation. Look for a church that faithfully incorporates only God's ordained elements into their order of worship.

God's Word Preached

Rather than "music-centric," a corporate worship service should be "biblio-centric." Alongside the preaching of the Word of God and the administration of the sacraments, the rest of the worship service serves to support and enrich the presentation of gospel truth and usher the congregation into the presence of God. As we will cover in the next chapter, the preaching of the Word plays a central purpose in drawing the hearts of God's people close to him. In the preached Word, the majesty of God is proclaimed and his precepts are made known.

In Acts 20, we get an insightful glimpse of the preeminence of preaching during a Lord's Day worship service in Troas, where Paul preached non-stop until midnight! A man named Eutychus will forever be remembered as the guy who fell asleep in church, resulting in his tumbling to his death from an upper-story window. Paul paused his preaching just long enough to raise him from the dead! Then without skipping a beat, they observed together the Lord's Supper, and Paul continued to preach until sunrise (Acts 20:6–12).

Music and Singing

What about singing? Although singing was not mentioned in the above gathering in Troas, we read elsewhere that singing is an important element in the worship of God. Paul exhorted Spirit-filled believers that they should be "addressing one another in psalms and hymns and spiritual songs, singing and making melody to the Lord with your heart" (Eph. 5:19). He added that this Spirit-filled singing should not be mindless songs, but songs filled with doctrinal truth about God (1 Cor. 14:15).

You might be wondering what style of music is most befitting to our worship of God. If you are to let God direct, you must be willing to set aside personal music preferences and sing that which is most acceptable to him! In Ephesians 5, Paul exhorted the church to sing a blend of "psalms and hymns and spiritual songs." A church should be willing to open up the inspired hymnal and sing from the Psalms. All 150 of these Psalms have been set to music repeatedly through the church's history, and these arrangements can be found in psalters or hymnals. Sing hymns of praise directed to God, not songs with more emphasis on us than on God.

Finally, sing *spiritual* songs; avoid churches that only sing songs that repeat light and shallow concepts over and over. Like candy, they might taste good, but lack the spiritual nutrition of richer, fuller songs and hymns.

Remember, the music of the church is not a matter of "contemporary" versus "traditional." Do you realize that all hymns that we label "traditional" were, at one time, contemporary? The great hymn writers of the past—like Martin Luther, Charles Wesley, and Isaac Watts—were the contemporary hymn-writers of their time. They all had one important thing in common: they penned beautiful lyrics that were rich in theological truth. The church should be willing to sing the songs from all generations of hymn writers, recent or past; this includes new hymns and songs whose lyrics are rich in truth and woven into contemporary tunes that ring joy into today's heart.

Look for a church that sings the great Christian hymns that God's people have historically sung through the ages. I would encourage you to avoid any church that is robbing their people of the rich heritage and blessings that come from singing hymns that were penned in past centuries. For example, you share in sweet communion with Martin Luther and the Reformation when you lift up your voice and triumphantly sing, "A Mighty Fortress Is Our God."

In summary, the music of the church is not anchored to the 16th century, nor is it exclusively contemporary or any era in between. May you find a church that regularly adds Psalms to its liturgy, as well as historical and contemporary hymns and spiritual songs that exalt Christ and bring glory to your heavenly Father.

If you visit enough churches, you will hear a diverse use

and non-use of musical instruments—from *a cappella* (no instruments), a lone piano, or a string ensemble, to a full rock band. Does God give any directions as to what musical instruments should accompany singing in worship? There are many instruments mentioned in the Old Testament including string (Psa. 33:2), wind (1 Kings 1:40), and percussion (1 Sam. 6:5). However, the greatest instrument of all is neither a pipe organ nor an electric guitar; rather, it is the human voice that melodiously expresses a heart redeemed by the blood of the Lamb. It appears that there is a degree of liberty as to what instruments may be played in the church. However, make sure that the church's use, or non-use, of musical instruments enhances, rather than detracts, from the singing voice of the worshipers.

Other Vital Elements

Worship also includes lifting our voices to God in prayer. Does the church you are considering incorporate prayer into its liturgy? Does the worship open with an invocation, asking for God's blessing? Is there a pastoral prayer where intercession is made for God's people?

Inquire whether the church regularly observes the ordinances of baptism and the Lord's Supper. While the Scriptures do not specifically direct us in the frequency of the observance of the meal of remembrance, a strong case can be made from New Testament—as well as church history—that the church has historically observed the Lord's table every Lord's Day. Whatever the frequency, our Lord knew that we have a great need to be often reminded of his death until he comes, and to celebrate the promises of his coming.

God gives the local church much latitude in how it orders the worship service; there is no set liturgy found in the scriptures. Other than gathering on the Lord's Day, there is no mention of time or length of the service. We already saw that, in Troas, Paul didn't stick to a twelve o'clock noon "deadline."

Let me close with a final exhortation: don't confuse worship with entertainment. Instead, look for a church where worship is marked by holy reverence, and where God's people worship in spirit as well as truth—a church where hearts are overflowing in joyful praise.

Questions to Ask

1. What elements do you include in your order of worship? How do you determine which elements of worship to include?

2. What guides you in the selection of music that you sing?

3. How often do you observe the Lord's Supper and Baptism?

4. How do you incorporate Scripture reading and prayer into your worship?

Digging Deeper

Chapell, Bryan. *Christ-Centered Worship: Letting the Gospel Shape Our Practice.* Grand Rapids, MI: Baker Academic, 2009.

Frame, John M. *Worship in Spirit and Truth.* Phillipsburg, NJ: P&R Publishing, 1996.

Ryan, Joseph F. *Worship: Beholding the Beauty of the Lord.* Wheaton, IL: Crossway Books, 2005.

Ryle, J.C. *Worship: Its Priority, Principles and Practices,* Edinburgh, Banner of Truth, 2015.

CHAPTER 6
Preaching the Truth

Preach the word; be ready in season and out of season; reprove, rebuke, exhort, with great patience and instruction.
~ 2 Timothy 4:2

As I ENTERED THE SANCTUARY of a church I recently visited, I noticed some striking aspects of the arrangement of the room. The pulpit had been removed from the church chancel (platform), and in its place stood a sizeable drum kit with a Plexiglas shield, a keyboard, three electric guitars, multiple amplifiers, speakers, and a half-dozen microphones for the worship team. There was no place left for the preacher to stand up and declare, "Thus says the Lord"—instead, he was relegated off the chancel to a nearby barstool on ground level. The service opened with forty minutes of non-stop singing followed by a twenty-minute "sermonette," filled with humorous stories and practical suggestions for Christian living but very little explanation or even reference to the Word of God.

It's not uncommon to find churches where preaching

plays second fiddle to music, and entertainment has replaced reverence. This diminishing role of preaching is nothing new; it was an issue back in 19th century Victorian England as well. An article entitled, "Feeding the Sheep or Entertaining the Goats," often attributed to Charles Spurgeon (but more likely penned by his student, Archibald Brown), loudly confronts the contemporary church's infatuation with entertainment:

> It works havoc among young converts. Let the careless and scoffers, who thank God because the Church met them half-way, speak and testify. Let the heavy laden who found peace through the concert not keep silent! Let the drunkard to whom the dramatic entertainment had been God's link in the chain of their conversion, stand up! There are none to answer. The mission of amusement produces no converts. The need of the hour for today's ministry is believing scholarship joined with earnest spirituality, the one springing from the other as fruit from the root. The need is biblical doctrine, so understood and felt, that it sets men on fire.[*]

As we yield to Scripture to regulate our worship, however, we recognize the centrality of preaching throughout the New Testament.

Think of worship as "dialogical"—i.e., a two-way conversation between God and his redeemed people: God speaks

*   Brown, Archibald, "The Devil's Mission of Entertainment," makingdisciples.net (http://makingdisciples.net/data/documents/the-devils-mission-of-amusement-archibald-brown.pdf, accessed August 1, 2016).

to us through the reading and preaching of the Word, and we respond through our prayers, songs and hymns of praise and adoration, the faithful observance of the ordinances, and heartfelt obedience. Preaching is the God-ordained means of igniting truth in the minds and hearts of God's people. Worshiping without the preached Word would be like worshiping in a spiritual fog; but when the light of truth is declared, the Holy Spirit lifts the fog, bringing worshipers face to face with the light of the Lord!

Through preaching, the lost are born again (Mark 16:15). Preaching is God's ordained means whereby the saints grow in their knowledge of him (Gal. 1:16), behold his mighty works, and are brought to walk uprightly in Christ-likeness. No wonder Paul exhorts young Timothy to "preach the word; be ready in season and out of season; reprove, rebuke, and exhort, with complete patience and teaching" (2 Tim. 4:2). As the beauty of Christ and his work and will are brought into brighter focus, the hearts of the worshipers are stirred up by the Holy Spirit with a renewed sense of wonder and praise, adoration, and obedience! If all of that is taking place through preaching, can you see how important it is to find a church where the pastor faithfully preaches the Word of God?

At this point you must be careful: in the same way that not all eating is healthy, so too not all preaching is profitable to your soul. A sermon filled only with stories, jokes, and pop psychology might bring pleasure to your ears, but it will have a deadening effect on your spiritual life.

I would encourage you to find a church where the pastor preaches expository sermons. Expository preaching follows the pattern of preaching employed by Ezra in Nehemiah

8: there we see Ezra reading, explaining, and applying the law of God resulting in the worship of God's people (Neh. 8:1–8).

An expository sermon begins in the pastor's study where he prayerfully takes a text of Scripture and thoroughly studies it to unfold its meaning. On the Lord's Day, he mounts the pulpit and reads the passage to God's people, and then unpacks the meaning of the Scripture bringing practical applications for the hearer.

There are great benefits for a flock that is being fed a healthy diet of expository sermons. First, it protects the sheep from a preacher's theological ruts and pet interests. Each sermon is anchored in the text, rather than the daily newspaper headlines or some other source. It is also a safeguard against doctrinal error, by unfolding rather than imposing the biblical meaning.

There is an added blessing when these sermons follow sequentially through a book of the Bible. God's people grow as they are fed book upon book, precept upon precept and line upon line (Isaiah 28:10). This approach to preaching brings the whole counsel of God to the church.

Another type of preaching is topical preaching, which can also bring a great blessing to the church as long as the pastor rightly divides the Word of God. This is a type of sermon where the pastor brings God's Word to bear on a particular topic of interest like, "How to be a Godly Mother" or, "Why the Attack on 9-11?"

Make finding a church with a high view of preaching one of your greatest priorities in your search for the right church. This will be a church where preaching is central to its worship of God, and where you will hear the pastor faithfully proclaiming God's Word each and every Lord's Day. A church where you and your family will be fed and grow.

Finding such a church will require a great deal of spiritual discernment on your part. You will have to listen carefully whether the pastor, as Paul described to Timothy, "correctly handles the word of truth" (2 Tim. 2:15). Listen for spiritual depth in the sermons. Ask yourself whether the sermons contain enough content to challenge you in your knowledge and application of the Word. Does the pastor uncompromisingly preach the hard truths, such as sin, repentance, and warning of hell? Are sinners being called to Christ and saints called to holiness? Are believers being reminded of how the grace that saved them is also the grace that sustains them?

Hopefully this demonstrates how essential preaching is to the life of the church—it is not an area you can compromise on, in your quest for a new church. The growth of your soul, and perhaps the salvation of your family, depends on it.

May God lead you to visit churches where you will hear the preached Word of God resonating throughout their sanctuaries and into the hearts of God's people.

Questions to Ask

1. What do you consider to be the central element of the worship service?

2. How do you select the Bible texts you preach on?

3. Would you describe your preaching as expository?

4. Do you preach the hard truths of the Bible? If so, which

ones and why?

Digging Deeper

Gordon, T. David. *Why Johnny Can't Preach: The Media Have Shaped the Messengers*. Phillipsburg, NJ: P&R Publishing, 2009.

Helm, David R. *Expositional Preaching: How We Speak God's Word Today*. Wheaton, IL: Crossway, 2014.

Millar, Gary, and Phil Campbell. *Saving Eutychus: How to Preach God's Word* and *Keep People Awake*. Youngstown, OH: Matthias Media, 2013.

Mohler, R. Albert. *Preaching: The Centrality of Scripture*. Edinburgh: Banner of Truth Trust, 2002.

CHAPTER 7
Church Membership

And when he had come to Jerusalem, he attempted to join the disciples. And they were all afraid of him, for they did not believe that he was a disciple.

~ Acts 9:26

PERHAPS YOU HAVE COME FROM a church background where membership in the local church was never taught, stressed, or practiced. You might be filled with questions: is membership biblical? I'm a Christian and have been added to the universal church; isn't that enough? Why do I have to add my name to a membership roster?

These are all good questions! It is true that, when God saves a sinner, he unites them to the universal church (body of Christ) (1 Cor. 12:13); it is made up of every believer—as the hymn writer poetically put it, "Elect from every nation"!

Membership Is Local

However, membership in a local church—which is also referred to as the visible church—is a commitment to join an identifiable body of believers. Churches without an identifiable membership are like a flock made up of unidentifiable sheep. No shepherd would attempt to lead a flock where the sheep would wander in one day to be fed, only to stray off to the neighbor's flock the next.

The biblical foundation for church membership is laid throughout the New Testament. In Acts 2, we read about sinners who believed, repented, and were added to the church in Jerusalem (a local church). They did not live out their faith individually but in community, devoting themselves to the apostles' teaching, fellowship, breaking of bread, and prayer (Acts 2:42).

Shortly after Paul's conversion, he went to Jerusalem. What was the first thing he did upon arrival? The Scriptures tell us that he attempted to *join* the disciples (Acts 9:26). The Greek word translated "join" is a strong word; it means more than signing a membership roll. It literally means to glue or cement together. It is the same word used to describe the permanent bond between a husband and wife (Matt. 19:9)—a bond that is so strong that our Lord would declare, "…Let not man separate it" (Mark 10:9).

Paul didn't enter Jerusalem to quietly sit in the back pew and just hang out with other believers. Rather, he sought to *bond* himself to the church at Jerusalem. Notice how the disciples responded to his request: they were afraid of Saul the persecutor, and didn't believe that he was a true Christian. In other words, there must have been a spiritual vetting process, wherein the church would hear the testimonies of new converts before admitting them into the flock.

Biblical Membership

What is church membership? It might simply be defined as: A Christian's formal declaration of commitment to a local body of believers upon the church's acceptance of their credible testimony of faith.

This commitment is reciprocal, wherein all the members enter into covenant with God and one another as they promise, by the grace of God, to faithfully and lovingly advance God's kingdom purposes for the local church. These purposes include: receiving the preached Word of God (1 Tim. 4:13); serving one another through the use of their spiritual gifts (1 Cor. 12:4–31); faithful participation in the corporate gathering of the church (Heb. 10:25); taking part in the ordinances of the church (Acts 2:28–42); joyfully giving to the financial needs of the body (2 Cor. 9:6–7); submitting to the church elders (Heb. 13:17); evangelizing the lost (Matt. 28:18–19); if need be, a willing subjection to church discipline (Matt. 18:15–20); and faithfully carrying out the many other "one-another" commands of the New Testament.

Declining Emphasis on Membership

Your search for the right church will quickly narrow as you eliminate from your list those that are not committed to church membership, as there continues to be a decrease in churches that embrace membership. Many churches have no formal membership at all; they don't require any commitment whatsoever from those who attend. Even in churches that still employ membership, fewer regular attenders are stepping up to make that commitment.

Why the decline? It's not that people are against membership per se; many of them have no trouble paying to be card-carrying members of Costco, the NRA, or making a more significant membership commitment to a club or group such as Rotary.

Part of the answer can be found in a lack of biblical teaching: many believers simply misunderstand what it means to be a member of a local church. Some think of it as nothing more than a denominational tradition, not something prescribed by God. To them it is more of a corporate requirement that allows them to vote at the regular business meetings.

However, there is an even deeper reason why church membership is on the decline, which can be summed up in one word: "commitment." There is something liberating about being free to come and go and take without making a commitment to others. Paul reminded us that the days leading up to our Lord's return will be marked by self-love (2 Tim. 3:2); those who abstain from church membership feel a freedom to take from a local church without a commitment to reciprocate in Christian love and service. When this happens, church takes on more of the character of a restaurant—catering to the desires of consumers—rather than a self-denying family of believers: it becomes a place where believers are free and willing to let someone else greet them, feed them the Word, clean up after them, and meet all of their demanding felt needs, at the optional cost of throwing some loose change in the offering plate.

The Vitality of Membership

How important is church membership? John Piper stresses that a church without membership is a contradiction to true Christianity:

> The New Testament knows of no Christians who are not accountable members of local churches in the sense that we have just seen. "Lone-Ranger Christians" are a contradiction because becoming a Christian means being united to Christ, and union with Christ expresses itself in union with a local body of believers. It seems to us that in the New Testament, to be excluded from the local church was to be excluded from Christ. This is why the issue of membership is so important.[*]

May God lead you down the pathway of self-denial, to a church where you can lovingly covenant together to advance God's kingdom purposes for his church.

Questions to Ask

1. Does your church have membership?

2. [If "yes"] What are the requirements to join your church?

3. [If "yes"] Does your church have a church covenant for its members?

4. [If "no"] How do you identify those who make up your church?

---

*   Piper, John. 1 Cor. 12:12–31, "How Important Is Church Membership?" July 13, 2008 (http://www.desiringgod.org/messages/how-important-is-church-membership, accessed March 13, 2016).

Digging Deeper

Eubanks, J.E., Jr. *Grafted Into The Vine: Rethinking Biblical Church Membership*. Oakland, TN: Doulos Resources, 2011.

Jamieson, Bobby, Mark Dever, and Jonathan Leeman. *Committing to One Another: Church Membership*. Wheaton, IL: Crossway, 2012.

Mack, Wayne A. *To Be or Not to Be a Church Member?, That Is the Question*. Merrick, NY: Calvary Press, 2004.

CHAPTER 8
Church Discipline

If your brother sins against you, go and tell
him his fault, between you and him alone.
If he listens to you, you have gained your
brother. But if he does not listen, take one
or two others along with you, that every
charge may be established by the evidence
of two or three witnesses. If he refuses to lis-
ten to them, tell it to the church. And if he
refuses to listen even to the church, let him
be to you as a Gentile and a tax collector.
~ Matthew 18:15—17

THE RIGHT CHURCH WILL BE a church that will love you
enough to discipline you when you sin. Finding such a
church might be more difficult than you think! Many
churches have bought into the common thinking of our
post-modern culture, based on perhaps one of the most mis-
understood verses in the Bible: "Judge not, that you be not
judged." (Matt. 7:1).

The church elders have been commissioned to shepherd

your soul—as well as the souls of your family, if you are married. They are charged with the awesome responsibility of bringing the flock to maturity in Christ. They will, one day, have to give an account for their faithfulness.

One of the God-ordained means of maintaining holiness in the body of Christ is through the faithful practice of church discipline. The objective of biblical church discipline is not to punish sinners, but rather to restore wandering sheep into a pathway of holiness. The great hymn "Come Thou Fount of Every Blessing" contains a sober reminder of what we all are: "Prone to wander, Lord I feel it." The neglect of discipline has the effect Paul wrote about: "a little leaven leavens the whole lump" (Gal. 5:9)—where the "lump" is the church!

How should church discipline be practiced? In Matthew 18:15–17, Jesus gives us four progressive steps for restoring a sinning brother in Christ:

- It must begin on the personal level. If someone sins against you, what should you do? Humbly go to that brother or sister alone and lovingly tell them their fault (v.15). If he listens, then you have restored a fellow believer.
- If the person refuses to listen, next take with you two or three witnesses (v.16). This is God's means to confirm the sin and the failure to listen. Hopefully, this combined confrontation will lead the wayward brother or sister to repentance.
- Thirdly, if the wandering brother or sister refuses to hear these witnesses, the matter is to be brought before the whole church (v.17). Not only should the church join together and pray for this person, but each mem-

ber should reach out and call their erring brother/sister to repent. But what if they won't hear the whole church and stubbornly refuses to listen?

- Finally, the wayward brother or sister is to be excommunicated from the fellowship of the church. Jesus directed the church to consider him as if he were a nonbeliever (v.17)—as one who is outside the warm fellowship of the believing church. Thus, church discipline is not only God's way of restoring sinners but it is also his means to protect the purity and testimony of the church.

The faithful exercise of church discipline is one of the sure evidences that the elders of the church love the sheep they shepherd. In Ephesians 5, Paul reminded us that Christ so loved his church that he gave himself for it. Why? "That he might sanctify her, having cleansed her by the washing of water with the word, so that he might present the church to himself in splendor, without spot or wrinkle or any such thing, that she might be holy and without blemish" (Eph. 5:26–27).

Questions to Ask

1. Is our Lord's teaching in Matthew 18:15–17 applicable to today's church?

2. Can a loving church discipline its members?

3. How does your church deal with members who are caught up in unrepentant sin?

4. When is the last time that your church practiced church

discipline? What were the circumstances?

Digging Deeper

Adams, Jay E. *Handbook of Church Discipline.* Grand Rapids, MI: Ministry Resources Library, 1986.

MacNair, Donald. *Restoration God's Way.* Suwanee, GA: Great Commission Publications, 1987.

Wray, Daniel E. *Biblical Church Discipline.* Carlisle, PA: Banner of Truth Trust, 1979.

CHAPTER 9
A Passion to Reach the Lost

Go therefore and make disciples of all nations, baptizing them in the name of the Father and of the Son and of the Holy Spirit, teaching them to observe all that I have commanded you. And behold, I am with you always, to the end of the age.
~ Matthew 28:19–20

IT HAS BEEN SUGGESTED THAT the local church should be added to the endangered species list. The rationale from a human perspective is that, without conversions, it is just one generation away from extinction!

Thankfully, God has revealed to us his heavenly perspective. Jesus Christ triumphantly proclaimed that *he* will build his church, and the gates of hell will not prevail against it! Christ entered this world to die for a people, and every one of them will be saved. He prophetically declared: "I lay down my life for the sheep. And I have other sheep that are not of this fold. I must bring them also, and they will listen to my voice. So there will be one flock, one shepherd" (John 10:15–16).

Jesus Christ victoriously accomplished his work of salvation on a blood-soaked cross on Calvary; yet, his work of redemption still had to be personally applied to each person that would be saved. What would be our Lord's means for saving lost sinners around the world? He commissioned the local church to go and boldly proclaim the soul-saving gospel. His marching orders were amazingly expansive: Make and baptize disciples in all nations of the world (Matt. 28:18–20)!

In your pursuit to find the right church, pay close attention to whether the churches you visit possess a passion to faithfully carry out our Lord's Great Commission. One of the marks of true spiritual life is spiritual reproduction; God not only saves sinners, but he also transforms them! With new birth comes a new heart—God removes the cold, hardened heart of stone and replaces it with a heart of flesh that beats with love for both God and neighbor. Therefore, true evangelism should be a delight that springs from a heart of love for our unsaved neighbors.

Be on guard for those churches that are unfaithful to our Lord's Great Commission. These will be the churches that are inwardly-focused and care more about their entertainment, yoga classes, coffee klatches, and youth excursions than the souls of sinners perishing all around them.

William Booth, the founder of the Salvation Army, had a passion for lost souls. It troubled him that there were so few that seemed faithful to our Lord's marching orders. He drew a graphic illustration of the state of the church of his day—one that is as relevant today as it was in the 19ᵗʰ century. He pictured a churning ocean with high waves, filled with people who were slowly drowning. Jutting out of the ocean was a huge rock, and on it was a platform with people who themselves had been rescued from the turbulent sea. They were within ear shot of many cries for help, yet, tragically, rather than going and rescuing those who were drowning, they remained on that platform where they were entertained with music and sat in stylish dress as they ate, drank, and were merry.

Look for a church where the saints are diving into the stormy seas of sin to rescue the lost. Any church that remains indifferent towards the lost and dying is one that is dying a slow death; it has become nothing more than a religious social society.

How can you recognize a church that is zealous to proclaim the Gospel?

To begin with, it will be a church that knows and embraces the gospel of Jesus Christ. That might seem self-evident; however, so often the gospel has been watered down so much that it has little good news left to proclaim. As J.C. Ryle put it, it no longer is sixteen ounces to the pound!

Listen carefully to the church's sermons and teachings for the Gospel message. Is it a message of simply asking Jesus into your heart, or is it a sixteen-ounce proclamation of salvation by grace through faith alone? You should hear of man's sinful condition and a warning about the eternal wrath of God. There should be a proclamation of the liberating good news of the cross, where the wrath of the Father was poured out on his Son on behalf of all who would come to trust in him. It should include the victory cry, "He is risen!" Oh, that you might hear a clarion call to sinners, that they repent and trust in Jesus as Savior and Lord.

Next, it will be a church where you will hear this gospel regularly proclaimed and expounded from the pulpit. Remember from chapter six: the preaching ministry of the church should be expository. It should have enough depth to edify and encourage the saints, but it should also evangelize the lost.

On any given Lord's Day there will always be a mixed gathering of believers and unbelievers. Frequently, God directs unsaved church visitors through the church doors. Snuggled up to believing parents will be their unconverted children. Often, too, there will be those who profess Christ with their lips but they remain in unbelief inwardly. They all have one thing in common: a need to hear the gospel of Jesus Christ proclaimed.

Third, this will be a church where the Gospel is faithfully being taken outside the church doors to their unbelieving neighbors. Inquire about the existence of church outreach ministries to the jail, college campus, nursing home, drug culture, or single moms.

Also, ask if this is a church that is committed to training the congregation how to evangelize. Evangelism is not the exclusive work of the pastor—it is the ministry of the whole church. When the Jerusalem church (all believers) scattered in the face of persecution following the martyrdom of Stephen (Acts 8), they all went about preaching the Word—and many were converted (Acts 11:19)! Peter exhorted the church: "But in your hearts honor Christ the Lord as holy, always being prepared to make a defense to anyone who asks you for a reason for the hope that is in you; yet do it with gentleness and respect" (1 Pet. 3:15). You will be blessed to find a church that is willing to equip you to effectively evangelize your family and neighbors (Eph. 4:11–12).

Finally, the outreach ministry of a healthy church does not stop at the city limits; Christ commissioned his church to go to the nations! The right church is an evangelistic church that is missions-minded—a church with a passion to send and support missionaries to every tribe, people, and language.

The need is great. There remains approximately 1.9 billion people in the world who have never heard the Gospel. Yet, there seems to be a shrinking interest in missions by many Western churches: the number of North American missionaries sent out, and the amount of money designated for missions, have both been in steady decline over the past three decades.* Look for a church that equips, sends and supports missionaries.

Be sure to add to your list a church that has a passion to glorify God by faithfully spreading his Gospel at home as well as to the nations of the world. It will be more than a church that has a world map in the foyer, filled with colorful push pins—it will be a church with a vision to faithfully fan the flames in the hearts of God's people, stoking them to throw out the lifeline of the gospel to a lost and dying world.

Questions to Ask

1. How would you define the mission of your church?

2. What steps are you taking to fulfill that mission?

---

*   Martin L. Klauber and Scott M. Manetsch ed., *The Great Commission: Evangelicals and the History of World Missions* (Nashville, TN: B&H Publishing Group, 2008). 128.

3. What gospel message would you present to an unbeliever?

4. Who are the listeners that you preach to on the Lord's Day? What message do you bring to them? Why?

5. How many missionaries does your church support? Tell me a little about each one.

6. What percentage of your church budget is allocated for missions?

7. What are you doing to reach unsaved people with the gospel in your community and region?

Digging Deeper

Packer, J.I. *Evangelism and the Sovereignty of God.* Downers Grove, IL: Intervarsity Press, 2012.

Tice, Rico, Carl Laferton, and D.A. Carson. *Honest Evangelism: How to Talk about Jesus Even When It's Tough.* Purcellville, VA: Good Book Company, 2015.

CHAPTER 10
A Church of Self-Denying Love

Do not merely look out for your own personal interests, but also for the interests of others.
- Philippians 2:4

IN THE JERUSALEM CHURCH THAT we read about in Acts 2 we find, on display before an unbelieving city, a selfless church whose sacrificial love for one another testified of their living faith in Christ. It's no wonder God was adding to that church daily those he was saving!

The church at Philippi was, in many ways, a good church that brought great joy to the heart of Paul the apostle. It would have rated high marks in each of the previous nine chapters of this book—but, there was one important quality missing: a heart beating with selfless love and unity! In Philippians 2:3–4, Paul wrote, "Do nothing from selfish ambition or conceit, but in humility count others more significant than yourselves. Let each of you look not only to his own interests, but also to the interests of others."

A Church of Self-Denying Love

Many of today's churches, like the church in Philippi, struggle with *selfishness* instead of demonstrating *selflessness*. Like chameleons, these congregations blend into the fallen world of self rather than standing out in contrast to the unbelieving world around them. There, worshipers are religious consumers who want to come, take, and leave unnoticed. These are churches where few heed Christ's call to deny themselves, take up their crosses, and follow him.

Search long and hard for a church with a selfless heart— if it is there, you won't be able to miss it: selfless love and unity shine so brightly that it testifies even to an on-looking world the authenticity of true discipleship (John 13:35). What are the defining characteristics of a selfless church? One Bible commentator has counted fifty-nine "one-anothers" in the New Testament; these are different ways believers are commanded to express their mutual, selfless love towards fellow believers—such as honoring, building up, encouraging, serving, and greeting one another. It could take years to observe the presence of all fifty-nine in the life of any church! However, here are four that should help you discern the spiritual heartbeat of selfless love.

Serving

Paul exhorted church members to humbly serve one another (Gal. 5:13). Twice, Paul reminded us that God has gifted each believer to serve in order to build up the body of Christ (Rom. 12:4–8; 1 Cor. 12:1–11). A healthy church is one where the spiritual leaders are faithfully equipping the members of the church to take up their spiritual gifts and serve one another.

You will witness this service when you see the members

actively doing the work of the ministry. What a blessing it is to find a church where the members are evangelizing, teaching, serving in the nursery, cleaning the building, and visiting those in need! Beware of a church where those in the pews more resemble out-of-shape, paid spectators that are quick to criticize the pastor—who is doing all the work of the ministry.

But, keep this in mind: like every other area of church life, this is one where every church is growing. Even in the best of churches there will be a percentage who are content to take rather than give. Lord willing, the churches you find will be ones where a growing percentage of the members are picking up the mantle of service.

Hospitality

Scripture exhorts believers to show hospitality one to another, and to others as well (Rom. 12:13; 1 Pet. 1:9). *Hospitality* comes from a compound Greek word that means "lovers of strangers." It is a disposition of the heart, characterized by receiving and treating guests and strangers in a warm, friendly, and generous way. Every time you visit a new church, *you* are a stranger! Consider whether you were received in a warm and friendly way—this might begin with a sincere, warm greeting, which later might lead to an invitation for a meal or dessert in the homes of members.

However, you mustn't be oversensitive in your evaluation; even the best of churches have an off-week. A church that is weak in hospitality should not keep you from joining. You might be the very one that God is bringing to strengthen the body in loving strangers.

A Church of Self-Denying Love

Giving

A church that is rich in self-denying love is a church that sees the needs of brothers and sisters in Christ, joyfully and generously digging deep to meet their material needs. We see this generosity displayed by the church of Antioch: a prophet named Agabus came from Jerusalem and foretold of a widespread famine that would strike Judea hard. Luke records that everyone in the church gave according to their ability to help relieve the suffering of the believers back in Judea (Acts 11:29).

A loving church will be one that is sensitive to the needs of the local body, as well as the greater needs of its surrounding community. It's a church that generously responds when a member faces medical, food, shelter, transportation, or any other necessary expenses.

Often, this sacrificial love reaches out to human suffering in all four corners of the world. Several men in our church were touched deeply by the cataclysmic losses in Louisiana and Mississippi from hurricane Katrina; they packed up trucks and trailers, delivering supplies, and took with them a crew that re-roofed damaged homes. When Haiti was rocked by a giant earthquake, killing 160,000 people and leaving 1.5 million Haitians homeless, another group gathered up donated hospital supplies and took them to Haiti, ministering with loving hands to the wounded Haitians. God used both of these opportunities to display the love of Christ and spread his Gospel.

Praying

What greater expression of mutual love and concern can there be than a heartfelt willingness to pray for the needs of one another (Acts 1:14; Col. 1:9; James 5:16)? As you visit churches, inquire whether each is a praying church. Look in the announcements for a prayer meeting, and attend them if they are offered. Is this a church that regularly intercedes for one another?

As some churches have become increasingly self-centered, there has been a corresponding decrease in church prayer meetings. But prayer is the life blood of a church—it is where a humble people cry out to God in worship and dependence.

You should make it a priority to search for a praying church. As C.H. Spurgeon summarized:

"The condition of the church may be very accurately gauged by its prayer meeting. So is the prayer meeting a grace-ometer, and from it we may judge of the amount of divine working among a people. If God be near a church, it must pray. And if he be not there, one of the first tokens of his absence will be a slothfulness in prayer."[*]

Questions to Ask

1. What are some specific ways that the community surrounding this church knows that you are disciples of Jesus Christ?

2. What are the ways your church displays selflessness?

3. What are some ways that self-denial is exercised?

---

[*]   C.H. Spurgeon, *Spurgeon at His Best,* comp. Tom Carter (Grand Rapids, MI: Baker, 1988), 155.

4. Does the leadership of the church regularly exercise hospitality? Would you share some recent examples?

5. How many members' homes have you been invited into for a meal and fellowship?

6. Who is the minister of your church?

7. How does your church put into practice Ephesians 4:11–12?

8. How are the physical needs of your congregation met?

9. When does your church gather corporately to pray?

10. How do you encourage the church to pray for one another?

Digging Deeper

Chantry, Walter J. *Shadow of the Cross: Studies in Self Denial.* Carlisle, PA: Banner of Truth, 1982.

Ryle, J.C. *A Call to Prayer.* Carlisle, PA: Banner of Truth, 2009.

CHAPTER 11
What Next?

*Not forsaking our own assembling togeth-
er, as is the habit of some, but encouraging one another; and all the more as you
see the day drawing near.*
- Hebrews 10:25

HOPEFULLY BY NOW YOU HAVE done your due diligence in
searching for a new church, mapping out potentially good
churches in your community, faithfully attending services,
and asking the hard questions. If not, I hope you are at least
in the process of doing so, if you have determined that you
have a good reason to seek a new church.

What's next? It's time to make a decision! If you are married with children, this is a great teaching opportunity for
the whole family: dads, I encourage you to lead your family through your decision process. Sit down together and
prayerfully evaluate the strengths and weaknesses of each
church on your list. Urge your children to see that your final decision rests on Scripture, not personal preference. This
will help them to know how to make this important deci-

sion in their own lives, as they become adults.

A Careful Process

Sometimes one church will rise above all the rest, making the decision obvious and easy; often, however, it won't be that clear. If you live in a rural community with only a handful of churches, you might be discouraged to discover how few, if any, of the churches in your community totally measure up. Typically in such situations, you are left to prayerfully select the church that comes closest to the marks set forth in the previous chapters.

Don't become discouraged at this point. The enemy is always nearby to tempt you to forsake church altogether. His twisted rationale goes something like this: "You deserve the best church. If the best church is not out there it would be better for you to stay home. After all you can listen to the best preachers in the world on the Internet. You can sing a couple of hymns, pray as a family and you are good to go about your Sunday business."

You might be wondering, what is wrong with this "stay-at-home" option? After all, isn't good preaching by myself better than attending a less-than-ideal church with others? The short answer is: no! The enemy's temptation is contrary to God's plan for his people. The writer to the Hebrews clearly exhorted us to not forsake the assembling of ourselves together (Heb. 10:25).

When we are alone and cut off from God's people, we are most susceptible to false doctrine, sin, discouragement, and a decline in our faith. In the Wyoming Mountains that surround my community, packs of wolves come down to the adjacent farmland at night, looking to feast on small herds of sheep. Their strategy is to zero in on one of the smaller sheep, cutting it off from the flock. Once it is alone, it is helpless prey to the teeth of the devouring wolves. Together there is strength! Remember, it is *together* that we provoke one another to greater love and good works!

There is truth in the old adage, *there is no perfect church.* I would encourage you to select a church that most meets the above biblical marks. Above all, this will be a church that most closely holds to sound biblical doctrine. Following your selection, make an appointment with the church leadership to discuss your desire or decision to join the church. Explain any differences you might have with the doctrine and practices of the church, and ask them if any of these differences would prevent you from becoming a member.

Don't Rush

Once you select a church, it might be wise to enter into a brief season of "courtship" before covenanting together in membership. This would include a limited period of time where you faithfully attend all of its gatherings including worship, Sunday school, prayer meetings, and any other mid-week gatherings. Use this time to get to know the people and continue to ask questions. A brief courtship may help you discern something you might have missed in your initial search.

However, don't over-extend your courtship. The temptation at this point is to enjoy the benefits of the relationship without making any commitment to join the church. I have known families that have avoided membership for years while they continued to wrestle over whether ours was the "right" church.

What Next?

Before you make your final selection, it is always wise to seek godly counsel. If you know a pastor in another community or a mature Christian friend, ask them if they would supply counsel in helping you discern God's will. They might bring up a perspective that you had not considered.

After that, it is time to commit! Once you know the people and ministry of the church, it's time to join the church. Become a good churchman/woman; take up your spiritual gifts and serve. You might be the very instrument that God chooses to use to have a new influence on its future ministry.

What About A Worst-Case?

There remains one important final question. Maybe you find yourself in whole-hearted agreement that there is no perfect church; you are even willing to join a church that best meets the criteria found in this book. However, after prayerful analysis, you conclude that's not a genuine option in your community—after examining the churches in your community, you found that none meet the above marks. Perhaps you have even concluded that the few that are present are so anemic in doctrine and practice that it would be spiritually dangerous to expose your family to their teaching.

What should be your next step? First consider widening the geographic concentric circles of your church search, extending it to nearby communities. You should be willing to drive, for your spiritual welfare and that of your family. We have had families in our church that have traveled as much as three hours each way for years, in order to join us for weekly worship. Although such travel is not ideal—and may be more necessary in Wyoming than in your region—it demonstrates how important a good church is to the Christian life.

What if there truly are no qualified churches within a reasonable drive of your home? Your options become more limited at this point. You could prayerfully consider if God might use you to help plant a new church in your community. I don't mean that you should start a church by yourself; rather, explore this option by contacting the closest good church to you, sharing your desire for a new church in your community. Our church has received several such requests over the years; we have faithfully explored each one, and it led to the planting of a new church in another Wyoming community.

Since even church planting is not always an option, I have saved the most radical step for last. If, after widening your church search concentrically there are still no good churches within a reasonable commuting distance, you might consider relocating to a community where there is a good church. Puritan William Gouge lamented in 1622: "There are many houses of God, places for the public worship of God, but yet through the corruption of our times, the ministry of the Word (the most important means of spiritual edification) is not everywhere to be enjoyed."* He went on to counsel that, when locating a new home, look beyond the presence of a view and good pasture—arguing that one should only settle where a good church may be found.

The modern outworking of Gouge's counsel is not only radical, but rarely followed. But God's means for equipping your soul for heaven is the local church; you should seek

---

* William Gouge, *Building a Godly Home, A Holy Vision for a Happy Marriage* (Grand Rapids, MI: Reformation Heritage Books, 2013), 239.

the presence of a good church in a community *before* you decide to relocate there. And, if you find yourself living in a community far-removed from a good church, you may well consider relocating your family. Several years ago, a family contacted our church about planting a church in their community. We faithfully explored that option, and concluded that God was not leading in that direction. The couple tried making the three-and-a-half hour trip each week, but adverse weather and other logistics kept them from faithful attendance. After much prayer, the couple decided that they would relocate, leaving behind their jobs and selling their house in order to move. God graciously provided an even better job for him in our community.

In summary: remember, the only perfect church will be found in heaven, where by God's grace you will spend an eternal Sabbath face-to-face with your Savior, and shoulder to shoulder with your brothers and sisters in Christ. Until then, identify the best church that is within a reasonable commute and join it. Covenant together to carry out God's will for his church. If you are in a community without a good church, consider relocating. Join your heart with Martin Luther and be ready to "let goods and kindred go."

May God wonderfully bless you in your search for the right church. Your spiritual welfare and that of your family depends on it!

CHAPTER 12
Are You Qualified?

And He put all things in subjection under His feet, and gave Him as head over all things to the church, which is His body, the fullness of Him who fills all in all.
~ Ephesians 1:22–23

IN THE OPENING PREFACE, I shared with you how my wife Mary and I had it backwards when we blindly embarked on our search for our first church home: we were looking for a church to worship a Christ whom we did not know in a saving way.

I don't think our experience is that uncommon. In fact, on any given Sunday, I suspect we all would be surprised to discover how many people march into the pews of local churches across the nation without having first trusted in the Lord Jesus Christ as their Savior and Lord. If you asked them why they were in church, their reasons would be many.

Self-Deception

There would be those who are spiritually deceived. They

faithfully attend church thinking they are Christians, but they've never truly come to Christ on his terms. They are like those Jesus spoke of, and about whom he will give this somber declaration on judgment day: "On that day many will say to me, 'Lord, Lord, did we not prophesy in your name, and cast out demons in your name, and do many mighty works in your name?' And then will I declare to them, 'I never knew you; depart from me, you workers of lawlessness'" (Matt. 7:22–23).

These are the ones who are quick to embrace all the outward trappings of Christianity—including church attendance, partaking of the ordinances, and other religious activities—without first repenting of their sins and coming to salvation through faith in Christ alone. They could be deceived by a hollow profession of faith that fell short of conversion. Their deception might come from a life-long family tradition of church attendance, or simply by some mistaken sense of cultural identity; there was a time in my life where *I* would have identified as a Christian because I grew up in America.

Self-Righteousness

There are others who view their church attendance as one big stepping-stone to heaven. Church attendance becomes one more filthy rag of self-righteousness they wave to obtain God's approval. They have a twisted understanding of God's justice as they hope that going to church will somehow tilt the heavenly scales in their favor.

Perhaps this way of thinking stems from bad theology learned as kids. I remember a Bible School "lesson" where we folded our hands, reciting, "This is the church..." (a building); then, as we popped up our pointer fingers we would add, "This is the steeple." Then we would open our hands, exposing our dangling fingers and climactically declare, "Open the door and see all the people!"

That lesson had it all wrong. The church is not a building or place; it always refers to a people. Our childhood example should be changed to, "This is the building, this is its steeple, open the door and see the church!" Yet, it is not just *any* people that make up the church, but a people called out by God. The term "local church" refers to a gathering of believers in Christ, who are uniting their hearts to worship, grow, and serve under the leadership of duly-appointed elders.

Bringing in the Lost

Although the church is made up of true Christians, God frequently brings people into the church who are spiritually lost, that they might hear the preaching of the gospel of Jesus Christ and be saved! This is what God used to save C.H. Spurgeon, who is sometimes called "the Prince of Preachers." During a brutal London snowstorm, Spurgeon ducked into a small Primitive Methodist Church for shelter on the Lord's Day. Due to the severe weather, the preacher was absent, and one of the faithful men in the church brought an impromptu message. He looked directly into the eyes of the young Spurgeon and cried out, "Look to Jesus and be saved!"

Spurgeon added, "There and then the cloud was gone, the darkness had rolled away, and that moment I saw the sun; and I could have risen that instant, and sung with the most enthusiastic of them, of the precious blood of Christ, and the simple faith which looks alone to Him."[*]

Over the years, I have witnessed many visitors and attenders whom God brought to our church because he was calling them to faith in Christ. A young lady called the church one Sunday after services, inquiring if we had any other services scheduled that day. She told me she was carrying around a heavy burden of guilt from her life of sin; she had attended three other churches that day, hoping that one of them would be able to show her how to be freed from her burden. Sadly, not one sermon pointed her to Jesus, so she began to call all the churches in town in desperation.

I informed her that we had no more scheduled services that Lord's Day, but invited her to join my daughter and me in my church office, where I opened up the Scriptures and pointed her to Jesus Christ, the only one who could remove her guilt of sin. I explained how his sacrificial death alone on the cross could pay her sin debt before God. I called her to repentance and faith in Christ to receive the joy of forgiveness and the gift of everlasting life.

She was noticeably moved by the gospel, so I sent her home that afternoon with an assignment to find a place to be alone, open her Bible, and begin reading through the Gospel of John. I told her that I would be praying that Jesus would reveal himself to her and bring her into his kingdom. I added, "If Christ saves you, will you call me?"

All afternoon, I was inwardly praying for her, and hours went by without a call. Late that day my phone rang; I could hear her joyful tears on the other end as she confessed, "He did it! He saved me! He has removed the burden of my sins!"

---

[*]   Spurgeon, C.H., *C.H. Surgeon Autobiography: The Early Years, 1834–1858* (Edinburgh: Banner of Truth, 1962), 106.

What about You?

Before you go any further in your search for a new church, let me ask this important question: are you qualified to be a member of the local church you are searching for? You must first be joined with the true church, the invisible church of Jesus Christ. It is often described as that mystical body of Christ made up of all true Christians—the church where all of its members have been born of the Spirit and brought to faith in Jesus Christ!

Are you a Christian? Have you come to Christ through faith? If not, let me share with you some great news: the Lord Jesus Christ, the Son of the living God, entered this world as a man to become the sacrificial Lamb. He offered up his life on the cross as payment for the sins of all who would come to trust in him. There on the cross, God the Father poured out his wrath on him—the very wrath that you deserved. The innocent died for the guilty, that your sins might be forgiven (Acts 10:43)!

Do you find yourself like Mary and me—actively hunting for a church without first coming to Christ as your Savior and Lord? Before this last chapter closes, let me call you to come to the Savior without delay. Do you hear his call to deny yourself, take up your cross, and follow him? Forsake your sins. Come to Jesus! There is no sin too great for him to forgive! He delights in saving sinners; the door of salvation has swung wide open. Come! The fountain of life abundantly flows; come and drink! COME! COME TO CHRIST!

About the Author

DONALD THOMAS IS THE PASTOR-TEACHER of Trinity Bible Church in Powell, Wyoming. He received a Master's Degree from Talbot Theological Seminary, and a J.D. from John Marshall Law School. He practiced law in California and served as a professor at the Simon Greenleaf School of Law. He and his wife Mary have seven grown children and eighteen grandchildren. Donald also authored, *What's Inside: Finding the Right One in Light of the Beatitudes.*

Made in the USA
San Bernardino, CA
05 April 2018